Your Own Stranger

Richard Miles

ONION
RIVER

PRESS

Burlington, Vermont

Onion River Press
24 Maple Street, Suite 214
Burlington, VT 05401
www.onionriverpress.com

ISBN: 978-1-966607-33-5

Library of Congress Control Number: 2025917019

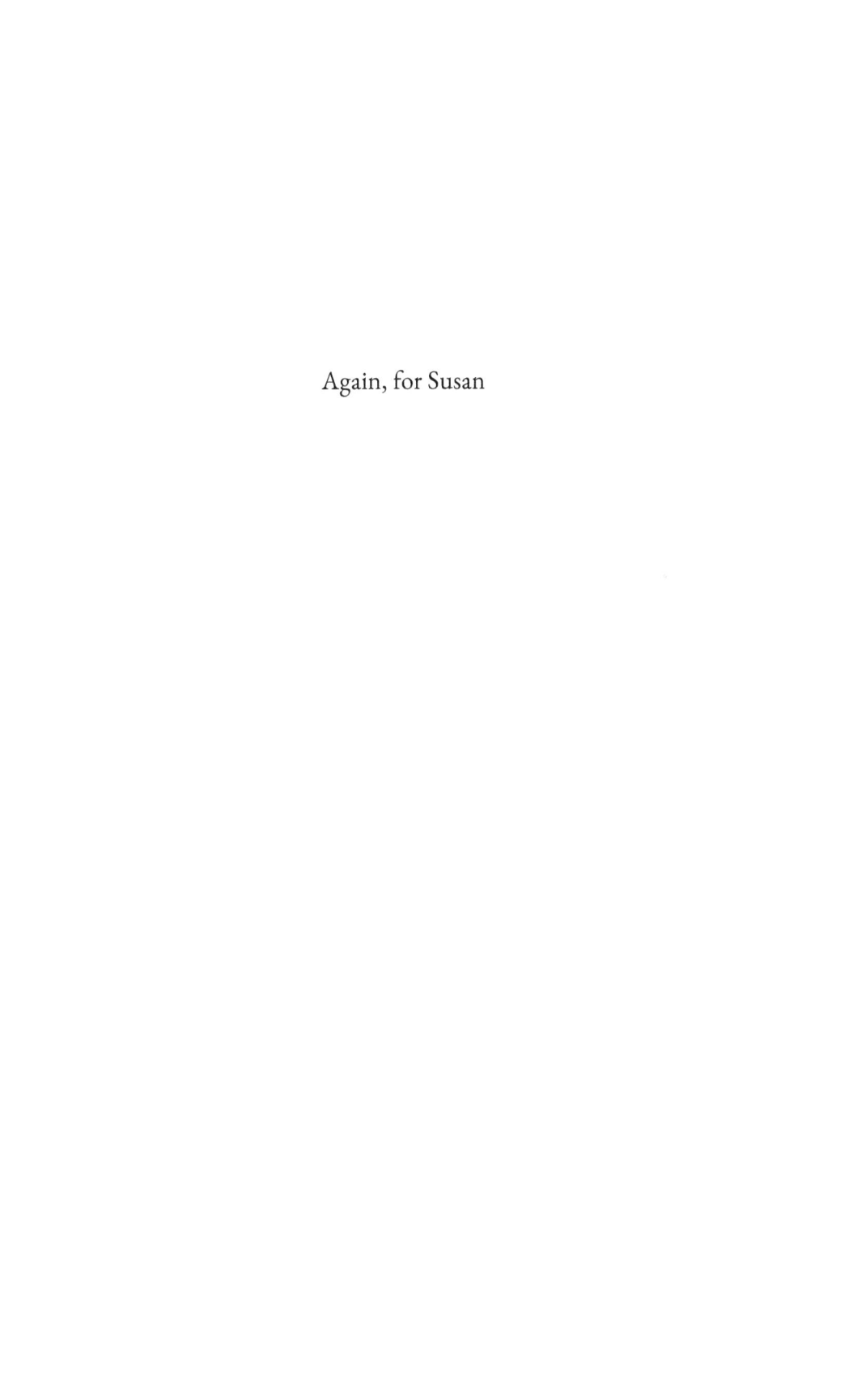

Again, for Susan

Acknowledgements

Grateful acknowledgment is due to the editors of the following journals in which some of these poems first appeared:

Barrow Street: "The Tears of the Fisherman"
Rustica: "Celestial Navigation," "Ghost Tree"

Contents

Part One

How the April day

resembles the ocean seething
in its own cauldron

and in two other cauldrons
a pond in the meadow
and the mind of a five-year-old boy

who discovers a blob of frog spawn
and the potential of worlds
resolves to an act of appearance

like his thought
a heron rises slowly off the pond
long and silent

towing its dripping legs behind
as if the pond were attached

Curing

A robin cures
on the sundial gnomon
watches time loan its shadow
to the moments
gliding off the top of her head
why look it's almost two o'dial
what to do
now which is next already
and what should I have done
or am I here a position
in being time

Cold Day in January

The bay carves itself
sun rolls slowly down the wharf
bending time
shadows of birds flash
across untracked snow
out of the blue
a knock on the door
it is the ghost
with distance in his face
with thorn trees in his eyes
barn door's unbarred he says
horses will get out
there is no barn
horses did not get out

Does This Tree Speak of Me

If I'm careful not to think
I may join without a self the chorus
of scarlet leaves
and acrid sweet decay
my health so well combines

a raindrop slides a spider's strand
or a spider seeds an earth with rain

Hang there like a fruit, my soul, till the tree die

writes Virginia to Thoby
over cold grouse and coffee
in her garden under the linden

and on the hottest autumn day
from my stomach
I withdraw a glob of heat
and watch it sickening expand

then from nowhere
the raindrop spider-fruitsoul
crawls up my bare chest
and pauses eye to eye
wondering if it will go in

I Was You

you let me out

with you in me
I feared not

we let ourselves
be stitches in the wild

Snow in May

Reeecharrr   Reee   charrr
a bird calls my name from an apple tree
born into blossom overnight   or is it a sole blossom
calling from the limb I sat on as a child
begging spring to return my mother to life

I trusted spring would
and knew it could not
but last night the moon's penumbra clung
to its vivid crescent
one contained in the other

the paradox embodied
where life is cast in all
its tumbling forms
to express the same thing
as in the flower's call   or bird's

and in this morning's shocking snow
ardent flake attached to each blossom

Doodling

By a stream with watercress
milling on its margins
we come upon a tall tree
its white trunk etched by a delicate drawing
the work of a tiny larva as it eats its way
through the soft tissue beneath the bark
a meander like our walk and for the grub
a map of its path of hunger

mid-way through its larval life the insect
turns and retraces its steps
devouring hormones secreted on the way
to complete itself it pupates
and flies away
unscripted as a moth

Glass Eels

To reach into the flashing churn
of urgent nerves
or catadromous elvers again
but which is which in this clutch
of clots unknotting in a pail

like a child in a twisted phase
fearing her own transparency
while for glass eels once larvae
spawned in the Sargasso Sea
it is camouflage

as the Gulf Stream sweeps them
over the continental shelf and they drift
into elver-size see-through fingers
and head for tidal estuaries
to press upstream against the salmon
their secret of bendable glass

where sweeping through fresh water
they're sought by my neighbor
toiling at night in the icy torrent
in waders slipping on slick rocks
to anchor his tunneled fyke nets
hub and spokes of a wheel of lives
some running with and others against the current
knocked hard by broken trees
and hearing the shatter in place
of living glass

Here

there are two places
and alert messengers in flight between them
are they the same moment
the body moves as a line through the landscape
while the spirit becomes the landscape completed
space itself is breath without boundary
absorbing the land from east to west
and the entire arc of sky
now the finest air made of particles of light
each a tiny center from which the whole is grasped
and from each vantage point above
we see ourselves approaching

Lot & Exp. – See Crimp
(from a tube of ointment)

January's lot that according to the bar code
of barren aspen stitching our field to the bay
will not expire until late March
when day less tightly crimps with night
and we start to see the dark
unravelling early along the ledge of sunrise
as it seeks a path home or forward
to release an abundant dissolve

Still asleep

the sun rises
leaves her bed
rests her cheek on the hilltop

listens as the slow tide
swings low slack to flood
its donning of silky breezes
stirs me awake

in the day's chill air
just enough to breathe
I watch the light spread
in a wide embrace

it is said that when you see
there is not a single thing

Autumn Equinox

I see the shadow of a crane-fly on the seat of a chair
and can't find it on the window for its slimness

when I do I lean close to the spot
on the glass the fly is poised behind

like rising beneath a water-strider
to flash a sticky tongue

does it notice
its wings twitch faintly

eyes in scale the size of my cheeks
antennaed proboscis stiletto I kissed

what does it know
along with the muscular crows talking in tree-tops

I step outside to sense
if what's coming is sinking in

as the fly sinks
into the window pane

a shadow of thought before it registers
or nearly lapped

Does it matter

that we are nowhere
even in the same house for years
just a moment then another
until we're here no longer

out in the field where crows are busy
elementary shapes of a child's drawing
come alive and intersect
and at sunset the air flashes
with tumbling knives

under all sound the rhyme of seasons rolling
undersound like a thought climbing to light
or the long voice of river beneath the ice
containing all the seasons
moving closer at night

Frog Time

A fat bullfrog squats in the mud
paradise of its own ongoing
where mud is all there is

I admire and absorb frog time
the long and handsome legs
it seems to know I could

watches me back
without a croak
or blink

Winter Breath

A doe masked in her winter breath
steps through a screen of shadow
onto a silent field
her shape sculpted in blue
and sets in the snow a silver necklace of tracks
lifting a dozen birds into flight

Dove's Word

Listen closely
the dove's word for rain

there it is again
and oh I do

sound like an aspen leaf
like my wing through grass

like my wound healing
like trodden grapes

and yes I know
how to think like a drop

that in dropping mimics
the dove's word for rain

a premonition
so what happens is memory

Part Two

Your Own Stranger

Howdy
where you from
where you headed
made in what aura

with no preferences
self-nourished and buoyant
like a raindrop or tree
with its hand or foot
in the earth

As a wakeful child

I stand in the dark
watching through the kitchen window
my young parents seated at the table
talking face to face

A world blooms around them
I do not hear their words
but the shadows of their voices
tell me I'm in their words

My mother rises before the window
trying to make out in her mirrored gaze
an answer from the depths of her life

She gives up
sits down again
then leaves to check that I'm in bed

I remember this years later
walking down the mountain road in Spring
into a sea of rising fragrance
when I nod to her father's ghost
ambling up the other side

Trail

Already there
beckoning from the wedge of sun
high in snowy mountains
a point years ahead

you know your path
leads through robbery
and hollow wind
in deep *springs of the sea*

with each step guided
toward the one already waving
from the glints of boulders

Your breakfast

no matter how you make it always
looks better than mine
and hints of Wallace Stevens this morning
as I watch two ravens ravening a rabbit cadaver
while smaller black birds in the field look on
and I "know, too,
That the blackbird is involved in what I know"
and that I too am not
as smart as a "widow's bird/ Or an old horse"

here in this house that hears summer's
footstep about to fall
the former and future moment
turns slowly in a benign long span
flattened against the green field
with lazy new tendrils to the kitchen
where all the windows are open

Someone Else

At the counter with my gallon
of raw milk the check-out person
asks why I would drink such a thing
I tell her my wife makes yogurt with it
Makes yogurt with it
she repeats
a murky concept
she hands me the receipt and mutters to herself
she senses an edge

In the parking lot a smiling stranger approaches
who greets me by name
Why it must be forty years if it's a day
You look terrific   how are you   and your Dad
You could be him again

I must be someone else
I say getting into the car

But it's got to be you
he calls as I drive away

In the interval between dropping a stone and your foot

the earth takes to its knees
and the sky deigns to notice before turning
its attention to an object falling
in a sequence of dead ends
taking their nauseating time
vertiginous in the middle
interminable to the toe
reversing gravity or gravity's other side
developing a taste for the dance
of realigning determinants
unmade remade unmade again
growing scales and feathers
a horrible enlargement of detail
universe in miniscule
lurches toward the far pond in moonlight
lightning charged ozone in the body
ferns growing out of it
and six dead languages in groans
all the forgotten messages of hindsight
that you were supposed to know
always too late
bonfire of errors
your humanness
on the ground to receive you

Grand Canyon

Had a body once
took it down Bright Angel Trail
to the Phantom Ranch

Ophthalmologist

My enormous head
clicks a lens in place
before one eye
I say x L v f z 3
unsure of v and z

Which is better
One (click) (click) Two
It's not an f it's a p and a capital B
(click) Three or (click) Four
Definitely Three I say as the letters shrink

I stare at a magenta dot
while close enough to kiss me the doctor
probes with his light-spear inside my eye
where I have never known it
much less entered

Within the space I came from
my eye turns around
and sees itself no longer
but seeing and object bundled
to fall again into

floating nonsensical signs
that cannot be read but swim
in the sea around my head

Sneak Peek

"...like turning up the gas quickly enough
to see the darkness" – William James

Seeking an independent view
of my mind so-called
slims it to a fleeing fish

when the real view
may resemble the expanding
night sky caught by surprise

squinting through a slip of crescent moon
just the seeing
unaware of what to see

like first sliding out into life
never to be separate from it

Floaters

The reached-for thing
eludes me
I find nothing

yet feel it
a phantom limb
a friend from far away

a floater in the corner
of my eye has moved in
a beginning or

resembling in indifference another floater
I sailed by in the East River years ago

it slides off then slips back

Crossing

There's a touch of licorice in the breeze, or waves,
or is it on the breath of the person behind me who says
It's a small world now, isn't it? and then,
That's salt air all right, good ol' salt air.
Faces of people long gone moil in the wake

and pinning the horizon I see that the speaker is right,
the world does grow smaller before my eyes—
a shrinking span, bridgeless water we cross,
and a future before us no wider.
We're just here, and then: here.

Last night I wandered home too late
after throwing all of myself, my whole life, into you
without a thought for tomorrow, which is today
and I woke to a pivotal moment
where another order, a primeval creature, slumbers in my heart.

It stirs and stretches
and this sluggish phoenix is me, too.
I watch it rolling in the wake
like a new ancestor, a coda
in the smaller world I am soon to walk upon.

Celestial Navigation

In the woods at night
the scrutiny of Polaris
is softened by leaf canopy

Where there is no path
I'm guided by the aura of trees
and I think of my father crammed with two other men
into a cockpit over the black Pacific
navigating blind by fixes on stars
with sextant and compass triangulating to a chart
suspended in lightless hours
physical location hypothetical
air and water one

After the war for the rest of his life
he was haunted by nightmares of missing
the speck on a chart
the fuel drained
his plane and crew diving into the sea
he bolted upright bellowing in panic

A staid businessman steady and calm
his nightmare panics shocked me awake
in the next room

The day after he was numb and cold
and as time passed
I began to veer off his course

He judged me errant
"in and headed for trouble"
but finding myself lost day and night
I was most alive and ready for anything
trip on a root and make a bed where I fall
adrift in the fragrant ferns

Grace Note

I've always been at home with illness
since life includes death why resist
and if they're inseparable
why not love both equally

I'll soon be better though perhaps not cured
for now I lie in clean linen afloat in fever
content and minus memory
with no smudges on my soul

Out my window the clear moments
land as common as birds in a tree
and resonate like a chorus
I wonder if there's a tone we're born to

A thread of the thread that does not seek
to verify itself in the past
so I need not ask what grace
and the note of the bird resolves

Sit down

you smell good tell me what news
you brought with the wind
the fragrance of my grandparents' granary
where the hen ate Gwion Bach as a kernel of corn
a story of transformation
not unlike the coals I stirred this morning
to open a warm mound of silence
disturbing two sleepers
who took my hand and made it their play
their voices lifted in branches
like the honeybee's cleansing flight on a warm winter day
the two departed and my hand returned   see
altered and pleased like you just home

Like water

we take the shape of our vessels
but why at times do I look away
with no idea where to go
and if I go somewhere
I'm longing for home

then sometimes
when the wind dies
shadows grow long and waver
their seasoned light capes my shoulders

and I blend with what I see
part of me watches the tide swing
and part goes out with the tide

Canyon Wrens

We work our way up the Gila River
cut stout sticks along the bank
to bat the yucca fiber ball upstream
letting it float back down to us

we gather empty clamshells in a basket
for our mothers to shape into ornaments
overhead the canyon wrens are gathering
excited they excite us

their cascading trills cast a net
and we are drawn
along a stream into a tributary canyon
where they dive into five deep caves

opened midway up a furrowed cliff
like huge dark eyes squinting into the sun
their deep shadow an invitation to join the wrens
as they stitch in and out of the light

the birds beckon us to follow
swooping over natural footholds
and loose stone our people might gather
for walls storerooms and walkways

within the open arms of the caves
we can see our families
held in a fortress safe from hostile tribes
and protected from the claws of bears and cats

the wrens' flight and landing
make their ledge a crystalline plate

for tiny steps on vermillion feet
and when they rest we lie down

beneath their ledges together
secure with water warmth and fish
living our dream with the birds
who have offered their home

By the time

you drive up the long gentle rise and crest the hill
through bars of tree shadow fluttering in your heart
you are so distant from your last self
it would be hard to say you were any different from this instant
blindly dropping into the unknown from the top of the hill
and somehow it's best to be no one
in this moment of being remade with all the force of falling

Part Three

Of our other senses

there is the instinct for beauty
arising from attraction or desire

which could lead to an illusory
sense of self
or isolation

a sense of direction and of the poles
as in bird migration which also demonstrates
the urge to unify in struggle

and to locate by dowsing
where placement and scale
provide equilibrium

there's the sense of *the thing in itself*
the tree or stone encountered
as body and mind

there's the momentary sense of a former
or future life
and the overlapping of tenses

as in the arctic tern's intuition of snow
her readiness in evolution
to become the color of her home

and seen in the many inviting roads not taken
each so difference-making as in
shall it be wing or hand

we bear alive in us traces of kinship
and guided by them
we call such promptings senses

Ghost Tree

I am not a ghost
but arteries and veins of wind
silhouette of anatomic whim

where are my leaves
but feeding birds whose flight
etched my bare limbs

and stopped in mid-air
where a branch would be

Under

Now we come
to under the day

sunlight chimes in the doorway
shadows crawl
in greens thickened to syrup

nouns come forth
with clear distinct voices
brightening ours

long bridges finding water
some early migrants
rest their span

Solitary oak

in a wide field
a star embering
these many years

absorbs each moment
appears always
to be where it is

for the first time
ghost
in its crown

What Might Have Happened

The moment arrives secretly
like a wound healing or like growing a tail
and we see it was there all along
two thousand twenty-four for example

Here's the hot breath of what might have been
bearing down a course of blind
desire and a chain of reckless leaps
ongoing where thought breaks down

so that if conceived
it probably caused its own conception
and now in this world where we can throw stones
as it grows dark and the maverick rain

drains down the wavy glass
where we doze on the porch under a light
we want to say to what might have happened
don't give up we know you're there you're always welcome

Corpse Rehearsal

"You tremble, carcass? You would tremble much more
if you knew where I was taking you."
—Henri de la Tour d'Auvergne, Marshall of France, 1643

You are no thing or character
neither block of wood nor hand of clay

now comes the hard part
be honest   unafraid to stink

no matter what anyone thinks
your odor is unique

so deconstruct
recompose

to the rock-hard
flash of light you signal from

An Accident

The footprints on the moon
are a stumbling coyote's
drunk from baying
who bayed with such passion
by accident he howled a word
meaningless to himself
though the cry made another coyote
and the two sang together
wandering in footprints over the moon
rounded in dust
like human ear shadows

A field away

I heard a girl's voice from another century
calling from the empty bathhouse by the stream
I could not see her but she saw me
the point of her voice forming and breaking apart
as the clouds overhead frayed and mended

A drop of water on her skin
what she said   her saying of it
like the exchange
between sunlight and leaf

When the skeleton

of a living stranger
whether ill or not
rose and appeared before her
she told her doctor who said
he could do little to alter
a prophetic course

now in crackling darkness
she stands before an x-ray
peering into the milky glass
her finely turned bones
gold chain afloat at her ankle
cherished flesh in which she shone
dissolved in grainy mist

upright and absent
she gazes through collapse at her white scaffold
hearing a distant piano
her head resting
on the shoulder of the stranger

Bones

of leafless trees and starlight
of spanning glances
animal bones prone on the ground
rise up and become a ship

bones of walks
of architecture
of bird and insect flight
the afterbones of travel

structures lingering most everywhere
snowflakes on eyelashes
pirouetting cores of thought
the bones of sound

and her silver bones grow long
in the body of her son

Tears of the fisherman

dropping on the ocean

    become fish

        swim into darkness

his great sigh

    a gust of birds

        also his boat

connecting two worlds

    raindrops bouncing on water

        a single bounce

and they are one sheet

    also his sigh

        and the Oh Well

his boat's name

    hand-in-hand with rain

        as he writes a letter

Aporia

She says Yes to another box
breathless yet to hit the ground
to see if she still lives

clothes torn and trailing behind
she steps into the box of a bus
from north to south toward the box of her job

holding in her lap the crossword box
where *curmudgeonly cries* intersects with *wonder cake instruction*

meeting of minds with *trouble's partner*

and *not conceal* with *multitude*

she stumbles to the back of the bus
into the box of a toilet
and pukes little cubes

hearing the song of the Cretan
who declares all Cretans are liars

Pond Life

On our walk we paused together
before the pond that swallowed a cloud

everything we knew
including what we didn't know we knew
had passed to the tadpoles

they are addressing the burning questions

as we sink
into mud and sky

Falling

Birds fly over
with their auguries
disperse catastrophes
passing above
stand back
a tree has fallen
into the sky in the lake
its fall still resounds
not the crash
the long fall
borne by its own weight
into a lighted sky in water
under and over

How shall we name this

that at once comes into being
and dissipates
shall we call it smoke
what color is it
does it matter   do we miss it
does it taste or smell
scare warm or move us
a recollection   a wish
is it a drug   can we eat it
does it need us
and now   and now
where did it go
if inside us
does it grow
by diminishing
a shadow   like an eclipse
in our hand

Part Four

A washed memory

of sunshine
gradually lifting the dim curtain
or is it your spirit lifting me again
to a buoyancy I can function in

In memory of Edward Fritz (1916-1996)

Psyche

Shadow on the face of the sundial
widening carefully like the expanding wing
of a butterfly just emerged
from its chrysalis its swollen body
pumping dyes into its wings
until in full bright sheets
it sails across the tireless day

Genetically Predisposed to Poetry

I have to tell you
the roosters have a word for it
the little fuzzies
in the midst of the drawn-out word they go
and forget
like scratching it out as they crow
and that's the word
scratch-a-doodle-doooo
genetically predisposed

as my lines no longer than the pad is wide
are not bad given a thumb muscle cramp
and my Spartan ways
these days when paths are covered with snow
what paths
and now there are paths in the snow
to render the old paths obsolete
a good thing
where might they have led to
but something is scrunching
step by step
and those are hinges swinging

I can see you there in that line
and keep you here in this one

My Handwriting

Moist track
of a blind snail

another life

navigating by hairs
in this one

The full moon

with a steady ivory gaze
sees clear into my head   down my spine
pins me to the ground

I look back at its many doors
and one by one begin
to discard inherited phrases

all I've said
without knowing what I was saying

Having mud-wrestled

with the poem
having touched the hollow of its thigh
pressed it to the ground

provoked its name
and at last put it aside

and months later to return
and find it breathing on its own
is it merely the residue of a day
part of the store of things

or has it spread throughout
beyond its making
an order forever altered
as on the departure of a loved one
or the birth of another

for Seamus Heaney, 1939–2013

The Poem Answers

I was there all along in the open field
scrambled in white, a part of your innocence,
the tenderest part, the simplest word,
innocence of the earth without the face
you sought within: *a silver trout*.
Fingers of your left hand rippled me,
I hid in your ear, the flame in your mind,
reflected your heat, was almost memory,

but like the *mountain grass* erasing the form
where the mountain hare has lain
I gave myself to the wind for you to hear
in the deep heart's core, and so was near.
Hiding in plain sight I was most in what remains
of your glance, a glinting hook in the dark stream.

There in the work

we perceive ourselves
viewing the work

our response
and what we've absorbed

come out of the work
as we go into it

for Jane Niebling

Translator

As I translate from my native Shoshone (in which my name Sacajawea means *Bird Woman*) into Hidatsa (where it means *Boat Hauler*), which my Canadian trapper husband translates into French, which then is translated by one of the rough men into English, I feel how lost is my word.

At thirteen two of us girls were stolen in a raid by the Hidatsa and held until the fur-trader won me throwing dice. Pain not only resists language but destroys it. My words circulating into space remind me of a wheel. The fight for survival names the natural world, which shapes perceptions and thought, which in turn shape language, and so around. My true language is geyser or river-rapid.

It is hard to know what is real
the men dragging their canoes
breast deep in the river
our bloody feet and hunger
or the mission driving us

this laughing broad-shouldered river mocks
my life and the journey
the expedition is my way out
my seat in a pirogue an eye
on what's inside me

what is the word that says bent into hooks by rapids
or the word for the mind's map unfolding
into unknown mountains

in Shoshone the word
for both crime and punishment is *lolo*
and the word for memory also means sky

to speak of the sorrow within
there is no word

I am in labor, in pain. Will I die? Captain Lewis crushes two dried rattlesnake rings into a sip of water. I drink and soon I give birth to a healthy boy. Who first had the courage to try this medicine? Now a mother I am more *Boat Woman* than *Bird Woman*. Or perhaps my truest name is "Carrying River", whose faraway source is deep within me. Call me "Far Away, Deep Within", like the origin of the words I seek to translate.

Up the Walla Walla we enter the land of many tribes, sometimes with twenty families living in the long lodge. Because I am a Shoshone woman bearing a papoose the people know we're not hostile. Though our message "had to pass through French, Minnatare, Shoshone and Chopunnish languages", I am proud to inform the chiefs "who we are, where we come from and our intentions toward them, which pleases them very much". One great chief, Hohastillpilp, said "he had opened his ears to what was said and his heart was glad".

To pass over the mountains we need horses, many of them. We learn that my own tribe has plenty of horses, as I suspected, but my people have withdrawn deep into the mountains. They have no guns and think we're a war party. I feel them watching us. After a few days we meet an old Shoshone woman with her grand-daughter, who is "Jumping-Fish", my childhood friend. We give them presents and explain our wishes and they guide us to my people's camp. My buried feelings erupt and flow. Tears are not separate words but a swollen river through breaks, falls and canyons. The Shoshone chief is Cameahwait, my own brother! We set up the tedious chain of translation but my brother and I read each other's thoughts and there are no words, only tears and laughter.

Two sisters

six and four
sense impending tragedy
and hand in hand are drawn

to the place it will occur
we see them etched in the cliff face
our shadow and our sun

Post Solstice

Days lengthen by seconds
beginning with the first

My time to live shrinks
by an equal amount

Balance in the suspense
of both at once

We descend the trail

where two clouds, one behind
and one before, merge overhead

the mountain casts its alpenglow

at the trailhead we sit with outstretched legs
cooling our feet in Frying Pan Creek

soon I will move into your sleep
where learning and forgetting are the same

my hand beckons, lights itself on fire, distant
ranges flare on your arm

No-one

Decaying leaves in rain
on the path to my cabin at dusk
a wave of sadness swells
through me like joy

wrung in a darker note
a no-one dazed by loss
my hand at the door
I cannot enter the dark room

unable to step out
into someone who fields memories
a husk on the steps
the night opaque

waves dropping to the shore
a breathing that could be my own

Kappatsupatchi

I am painting a pond
on top of a mountain
I'm here every day

I'm getting close
there it goes
start over again tomorrow

sick of climbing
forget I'm climbing
until on top awash

the water-eye
trusts the unseen
to come through me

and then again differently
until one morning
I've about given up

a fish leaps
looks around
splashes down

No wind

does not mean
windless

it means
yes, wind

Notes

"Does this tree speak of me" (p. 14)
The italicized line is from Shakespeare's *Cymbeline*, Act V, Scene V.

"Trail" (p. 31)
springs of the sea is from Job 38:16

"Your breakfast" (p. 32)
Both quotes are from Wallace Stevens poems. The first, from "Thirteen Ways of Looking at a Blackbird"; the second, from "Nuances of a Theme by Williams".

"Sit down" (p. 43)
Gwion Bach is a character in a legendary tale of the Welsh bard, Taliesin.

"Corpse Rehearsal" (p. 56)
The epigraph is a remark made on the battlefield by Henri de la Tour d'Auvergne, Vicomte de Turenne, Marshal of France, in 1643.

"The Poem Answers" (p. 75)
innocence of the earth is from Wallace Stevens' "Auroras of Autumn"
a silver trout, is from Yeats' "The Song of Wandering Aengus"
the mountain grass and *where the mountain hare has lain,* are from Yeats' "Memory"
in the deep heart's core, is from Yeats' "The Lake Isle of Innisfree".

All the quotes in "Translator" (p. 77) are from *The Journals of Lewis and Clark*.

Kappatsupatchi (p. 83)
This word is onomatopoeic in Japanese for a fish leaping from the water and splashing down, and is associated with complete integration.

Photo: Nathan Hendrie

Richard Miles' poems have appeared in various publications and journals, including *The New Yorker* and *The Beloit Poetry Journal*. His previous books are *Boat of Two Shores*, *Child*, and *Alight*. He is a retired stonemason and sculptor in stone. He lives with his family on the coast of Downeast Maine, near a lighthouse, The Nash Island Light, which he and his family and friends restored.

www.ingramcontent.com/pod-product-compliance
Lightning Source LLC
Chambersburg PA
CBHW051329120626
46547CB00016B/2465